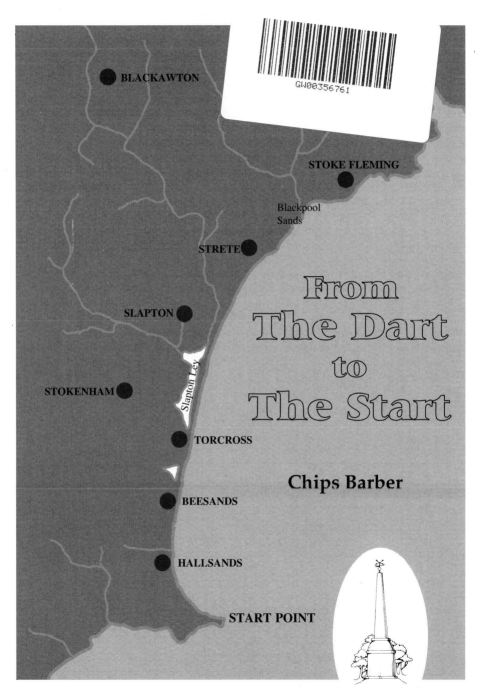

BLACKAWTON

STOKE FLEMING

Blackpool
Sands

STRETE

SLAPTON

Slapton Ley

STOKENHAM

From
The Dart
to
The Start

TORCROSS

Chips Barber

BEESANDS

HALLSANDS

START POINT

OBELISK PUBLICATIONS

ALSO BY THE AUTHOR

Diary of a Dartmoor Walker • Diary of a Devonshire Walker
The Great Little Dartmoor Book • The Great Little Totnes Book
The Great Little Plymouth Book • Plymouth in Colour
Dark & Dastardly Dartmoor • Weird & Wonderful Dartmoor
Ghastly & Ghostly Devon • Haunted Pubs in Devon
Dartmouth and Kingswear • The South Hams in Colour
Film and TV Programmes…Made in Devon • The Dartmoor Quiz Book
Ten Family Walks on Dartmoor • Six Short Pub Walks on Dartmoor
Newton Ferrers and Noss Mayo
Around & About Burgh Island and Bigbury Bay
Around & About Hope Cove and Thurlestone
Place Names in Devon • An A–Z of Devon Dialect
Colourful Dartmoor • The Story of Hallsands
Devon's Railways of Yesteryear • Along The Avon
Walk the South Hams Coast–Dartmouth to Salcombe

OTHER TITLES ABOUT THIS AREA

Under Sail Through South Devon & Dartmoor, *Raymond B. Cattell*
Haunted Happenings in Devon, *Judy Chard*
The Ghosts of Berry Pomeroy Castle, *Deryck Seymour*
Walks in the South Hams, *Brian Carter*
The Ghosts of Totnes, *Bob Mann*
The Dartmoor Mountain Bike Guide, *Peter Barnes*
Walks in the Totnes Countryside, *Bob Mann*
Dart Country, *Deryck Seymour*
Murders and Mysteries in Devon, *Ann James*
Circular Walks on Eastern Dartmoor, *Liz Jones*
Dartmoor Letterboxing for Beginners, *Kevin Weall*
Beesands and Hallsands of Yesteryear, *Cyril Courtenay*
Beesands and Torcross of Yesteryear, *Cyril Courtenay*
Churches of The South Hams, Parts One and Two, *Walter Jacobson*
Villages of The South Hams, *John Legge*
We have over 180 Devon-based titles; for a list of current books please send SAE to
2 Church Hill, Pinhoe, Exeter, EX4 9ER or telephone 01392 468556

Plate Acknowledgements:
Thanks to Mr Cleave for pages 7, 15, 17 (bottom), 31 and 32.
Cyril Courtenay for pages 22 (top), 23 and 24 (top). D. Cox for page 14.
All other photographs are by or belong to Chips Barber

First published in 1994, reprinted in 2003 by
Obelisk Publications, 2 Church Hill, Pinhoe, Exeter, Devon
Designed and Typeset by Sally Barber
Printed in Great Britain

From The Dart to The Start

In travelling westwards across South Devon, once the Dart is crossed, the countryside and coastline assumes a special, almost magical atmosphere. This is the South Hams, and the coastline of Start Bay is a majestic sweep from the mouth of one of Devon's main rivers southwards to one of its most striking headlands. "From The Dart to The Start" is Devon at its very best but we shall discover, as we venture forth along this southern seaboard, the area has also witnessed heartaches, hardships and harrowing stories. However, those who live there would never want to leave and there are thousands of people who make an annual pilgrimage from the concrete jungles of our mega city conurbations who would gladly stay on if the circumstances permitted. Maybe this little book will warm their hearts and revive their spirits when they are in exile from this magical land.

We will begin along those amazing cliffs that clamber out of the mouth of the Dart not far from Dartmouth's very impressive little castle. These days it is the done thing to walk the coastline. We are an island race and seem obsessed with the notion of patrolling, in pedestrian fashion, this interface of cliffs and coves, bays and beacons, wind and waves. If you want to get away from it all, this coastline is not the place for it as so many folk stalk along it each day, even in winter. They do so because it's there and because it's indescribably beautiful. Even the names are evocative as the mouth of the Dart gets left behind – Deadman's Cove and Compass Cove – like names out of some cleverly concocted novel, maybe Agatha Christie, who lived not far from here as the seagull flies, at Greenway on the far side of the River Dart.

Beyond Combe Point are the sharp pinnacle-like rocks called the Dancing Beggars. They featured in a wonderful book about this area called *Under Sail Through South Devon and Dartmoor*. Originally written in the mid 1930s it's the story of an adventurous journey around the south coast of Devon, by a young man, with various companions for different sections of the voyage, by canoe. When he got as far up the creeks and rivers of South Devon as his small boat would allow, he walked on over the hills. That way he managed to reach Dartmoor as well. The author, Professor Raymond B. Cattell, is literally a genius and that is a fact rather than an opinion! This is an extract of his encounter, in the

1930s, with Combe Point and the awesome Dancing Beggars.

In less than an hour from Totnes we passed between the castles (at the mouth of the Dart), out to the blue and the burnished gold of a calm, sunbathed sea.

Sandpiper immediately turned her nose southward, as if she knew of fair coasts awaiting her, and we paddled on by cliffs and lofty hillsides of wild loveliness.

A mile further our attention was caught by a white cross gleaming on the cliff face of a small, inaccessible cove. Jean's curiosity, and my desire for a respite from being knocked on the head by her paddle, combined to bring us swiftly to the shore. We found the strange object to be a marble cross to the memory of one Christopher Reade, I believe, who fell from the cliff above and whose dying words, "It's all right", were recorded on this stone. Perhaps these are meaningless, automatic words of a semiconscious man or perhaps, uttered at this shrine of rare beauty, they express the profoundest philosophy of life and death.

We were somewhat silent for a time but soon, such is the unteachable self confidence of man, I conceived a desire to climb the cliff to get a photograph of the cove. I considered sufficient respect was paid to the gruesome reminder on the cliff face if I climbed the opposite wall. Having got my photograph I began the descent but on a scree my foot slipped and I came bounding down. Somehow I managed to avoid a direct hit from the jagged rocks and even kept the camera safely clutched in my hand, but at the bottom of the scree, just as I was coming to rest, a veritable spear of rock more cunning or malevolent than the rest penetrated my guard and stabbed me in the small of the back. The camera crashed on the beach...

For myself, I tottered to the boat, but my paddling, in virtue of my bruised spine, was even more erratic than Jean's and I knew we shouldn't get much further that day.

In this fashion we reached Combe Point and passed through an archipelago of jagged rock pinnacles slanting out of the water at crazy angles. They are called The Dancing Beggars and very drolly do they suggest a group of dancing, tattered humans. Not content with the recent experience I climbed on one of these to photograph Jean amidst them. We were both somewhat nervous, however, Jean because it was the first time she had been left to manage a boat alone and I because if she failed to get me aboard again I was doomed to spend the rest of my days sitting on a very spiky dancing beggar. Fishermen who meet The Dancing Beggars in bad light and with an onshore wind are apt to mispronounce their title, I am told.

But if you want to find out if Ray Cattell is still marooned on that rock or whether he managed to continue on his voyage along Start Bay, then you will have to read his marvellous book!

Redlap Cove lies between Warren Point and Stoke Fleming. It was the scene of a bizarre sighting many years ago...

The local press went to great lengths to convince the public that Mr Groves, head gardener of the famous actor, Cyril Maude, was an honest man beyond reproach. By doing so they added an air of credibility to an incredible episode. The man was 'strictly temperate' and was 'a very observant and reliable man'. It usually mattered not whether someone was given to the odd tipple or was capable of a few white lies. But in this case it had to be established that Mr Groves was a genuine sort as the water-borne 'monster' that he saw defied belief and he was the only man who saw it... The press published this as part of their account of the proceedings in January 1937.

Unlike those who say they have seen the Loch Ness Monster, Mr Groves, whilst enjoying a spot of fishing, at Redlap Cove just east of Stoke Fleming, was close to his unexpected quarry. He was near enough to see the monster's head in photographic detail. So we get a remarkable picture of this composite creature with a sheep's head and a camel's jaws; clean shaven features and a solitary tuft at the top like a last stronghold defying the siege of baldness; bulging eyes but no ears.

The description then added that the creature had humps like a camel. In all he watched the creature swim around for some thirty seconds before it submerged not to resurface again. However if you read *Around and About Salcombe* you will see that this monster was not averse to trying other coastal inlets or locations in those prewar years...

Stoke Fleming's Church tower stands boldly against the skyline when seen from the sea. For this reason, in the past, it was used by vessels bound for Dartmouth as a navigation aid. They say that in the days of smuggling, luggers intending to bring contraband into nearby Blackpool Sands waited a short way offshore until they spotted a red light on Stoke Fleming's church tower giving them the go-ahead to land.

The church tower's uprightness and height have made it an obvious target for lightning bolts. In January 1880 it was struck by one and the immediate impression witnesses had to the severity of the strike was that it would cost a fortune to repair the damage. However, when they looked more closely it was discovered that the mighty flash had inflicted less damage than was thought, the bill being about one eighth of their expectation.

In its long history it has had many colourful rectors. Richard Raynolds would rank as one of the adventurous ones. The English Civil War (1642–1646) took place during his incumbency and he was turned out of his beloved church – at the age of eighty! However, he was built of rock more resilient than even the local Dartmouth slates and resumed his post at the cessation of hostilities. His durable constitution saw him live until he was nearly one hundred years old.

Buried at Stoke Fleming is the second genuine genius that we encounter in this book – George Parker Bidder (1806–1878). His abilities were of the mathematical type with a mind able to encompass sums that most mortals would struggle to perform today even with the help of a calculator or a computer.

George grew up at Moretonhampstead on the edge of Dartmoor. He had exceptional ability that lead him to work with the greatest engineering minds of his day. Railway engineer, George Stephenson, was a great friend, the two of them heavily involved in pioneering railway projects. Had he been alive today he could have applied his considerable brain to improving the traffic flow through this often congested village. He invented the swing bridge, having introduced the first one seen in this country on the Norwich & Lowestoft Railway. For good measure he also constructed London's Victoria Docks but his fame was derived from his powers of mental agility. He could add enormous columns of numbers or multiply large sums in his head and his memory for numbers was exceptional. His father knew that this was a rare gift and made money out of his genius son. He was so adept with statistics that he served on Parliamentary committees examining finances; by simply running his eye down a column of facts and figures he

could spot irregularities or mistakes in an instant!

A memorial was unveiled at Stoke House in May 1940 to honour his achievements. Although he never lived there his family spent some seventy years there. The memorial was erected by a distant relative, Captain Willcox, and unveiled by the oldest Stoke Fleming-born resident, Mrs S. A. Shepherd.

It is hard to imagine but the beautiful Blackpool Sands, as far removed in appearance from its Lancastrian namesake as one could get, is a place that has witnessed bloodshed on many occasions.

In 1404 a force of more than 2,000 Bretons landed at Slapton Sands intent on surprising, then burning Dartmouth to the ground. They were well practised having caused considerable damage and mayhem in Plymouth the autumn before. Their leader was Lord Du Chatel who thought that an approach on land along the coast would have the surprise element needed to give them the upper hand. However the English were wise to the attack and some 600 men, and many fired-up women, gathered at Blackpool for the confrontation.

In those days it is more than likely that this was a tidal inlet rather than just a sandy cove with a trickling stream percolating its way to the sea at the southern end of the beach. With a high tide this creek's waters would have been deep enough to have been a considerable obstacle, and so it proved.

The Breton forces were lacking the crossbowmen necessary to give cover for the knights. These heavily-weighted fighting men had underestimated the depth of waters in the inlet and foundered whilst showers of arrows rained down on them. The enemy beat a retreat. Some reckon that Du Chatel had a fortune with him on this mission but as things got tough he sought out a woody glade and buried it there, not far from Blackpool Sands. As it has never been found there may be buried treasure somewhere in these parts. Du Chatel was killed soon after!

The closest people have got to finding treasure, so far, is the discovery, early in the twentieth century, of gold coins from the time of Richard II. The source of these valuable coins stems from ships returning to Dartmouth but driven ashore by French vessels in hot pursuit.

In the Domesday Book it records 'Em' as a place to tie up boats. Today we have Embridge about half a mile up what was probably a tidal creek in the past.

An old picture postcard view of Stoke Fleming

With such a long coastline, the threat of invasion was a constant one. Henry VIII was well aware of the possibilities. He was keen to see a castle built at Blackpool Sands to help protect Dartmouth, a major port in those days. However this never materialised, apart from a bulwark that was manned between 1554–1599. The last date was significant as there was a real worry about an invasion that year and hundreds of men alerted throughout the region made their way to the coast. What better place to be stationed, for a false alarm, than Blackpool Sands?

Since the last ice age sea levels have fluctuated but with a trend towards rising. Therefore features once on the shoreline have been submerged. This is the case at Blackpool Sands where there are the remains of a submerged forest. When certain conditions prevail the stumps of some of the trees can be seen. Arborealists have identified various species here such as oak and cedar. They have also found various cone-bearing trees, which is not surprising as part of the attraction of this inlet today is its wooded backcloth. It's far more sylvan than any of the other beaches, found to the south, along the Start Bay shoreline.

As we shall see in greater detail later, this coastline has suffered at the hands of the sea, sometimes by purely natural forces but sometimes with a little unwitting help from the hand of Man. Blackpool has had its beach battered by storms and its cliffs undermined by the wind and sea. A 12 foot high and 6 foot wide sea wall was built to keep the elements at bay between 1860–1873. But it's almost as if the sea rises to a challenge and those objects placed in its path immediately attract its unwanted attention. Consequently the eastern end was largely destroyed in February 1917, whilst land and trees were washed away in 1925 and 1929. But even then the sea's relentless work wasn't done for it attacked again in dramatic fashion in both 1930 and 1933. Indeed the storm damage of 1930 left the beach looking like a battlefield with large bits of the masonry defences, or what remained of them, left strewn all over it. A large part of a field adjoining the beach was washed away and a boathouse, which had been constructed safely in the middle of it, now teetered precariously on the seaward edge.

At the end of the 1980s a large section of cliff subsided severing the coastal road link. This had devastating effects on the local economy, a situation only remedied after a period of many months by a lot of skilled construction work. The A379 was eventually shored up to allow life to begin again for the traders of the district.

Despite the ongoing problems of seasonal storms and their attendant problems, various film makers have made full use of better weather to make many films in this South Hams paradise. *The Sea Hawk* (1919), *The Written Law* (1932) and *The Wonderful Story* (1933) all used Blackpool Sands.

This beach and nearby Redlap Cove were ideal for filming some of the scenes for the 1930 Associated British Screen adaptation of Neville Shute's *The Lonely Road*. The general production manager, Wilson Blake, was no stranger to Devon having been here to shoot *Escape* on Dartmoor and *Lorna Doone* on Exmoor. Working on the assumption that he liked to make a film where a book had been set, he knew that Neville Shute had this area in mind when he had written this novel.

In those halcyon days of the British film industry, money was no problem and about sixty people descended on Dartmouth in June to fill two hotels for a period of several days. The stars of this film were Clive Brook, who had the leading male role and his leading lady, Victoria Hopper. The co-stars included Charles Farrell, Malcolm Kean and Dennis Wyndham.

In June 1991 Emma Thompson and Anthony Hopkins came to Blackpool Sands to shoot some sequences for an adaptation of E.M. Forster's novel *Howard's End*. Although the weather wasn't as fine as the film makers would have liked, the stars were quite happy to be in such a beautiful location.

But there have been many stars here and even more films made in this lovely little bay. A veritable galaxy of international stars have graced these sands and the surrounding headlands at various times. If you want to find out about more then you should read *Made in Devon*, which deals with a vast number of small and large screen productions made in this fair county. Nearby Dartmouth could almost claim to be 'The Hollywood of England'.

Blackpool Sands remains a favourite place for many people with its quaint toilet block and, even more unusual, pink telephone box.

Some say that flotsam and jetsam are the harvests of the sea and some unusual items have found their way onto the Start Bay shoreline at times. The enormous jawbone of a whale was discovered at Blackpool Sands many years ago. There was some talk of erecting it as a gateway, as they had done at Teignmouth long ago, but this never happened here.

For those who indulge in trivia – Did you know that the last stage coach ever held up, by a highwayman, in this country was at Blackpool Sands? It happened in the 1870s but,

From The Dart to The Start

although the stage coach was loaded down with loot in the form of thousands of pounds worth of silver coins, the highwayman was thwarted, leaving empty handed. Mr Sanders was the driver, pulling up when he heard screams coming from the lady passenger inside. A hand had opened the door and was foraging about in search of the cash box. Little did the highwayman know but the box had been placed in the boot. Mrs Elliot's piercing screams frightened off the would-be robber. This attempted highway robbery was on one of Vickery and Tucker's coaches, which operated a twice-daily stage coach service between Kingsbridge and Dartmouth. Incidentally, Mr Vickery also owned the Tor Cross Hotel.

History relates that Mrs Elliot, the wife of a local doctor, was no stranger to such incidents. On an earlier occasion, in the same coach but at Chillington, she was a passenger sitting beside the coachman. A pistol appeared over an orchard wall and was fired at the stage coach. The bullet whizzed between them but, apart from being badly shaken, both were unhurt. After this close scrape she wisely chose to ride inside where there were yellow corduroy cushions on which to sit.

There were other problems in this area. The route along the top of the shingle ridge of Slapton Sands was a vast improvement to the original roller-coaster inland route through a maze of narrow, often swampy lanes. But the road beside the leys was an exposed one and the stage coaches lacked the bulk to withstand onshore gales. To overcome this acute problem when such conditions prevailed with the winds blasting in over Start Bay, the coach would make its usual stop at Torcross when Dartmouth-bound. Here it would take on heavy stone ballast to give the vehicle the weight needed to combat the stormy winds. On successfully negotiating this open and exposed stretch, the stone was deposited at Strete Hill where it could be used by the next conveyance going back to Torcross, Kingsbridge-bound. Those coaching days persevered longer in remote areas like this, away from the network of the railways, than in other areas.

Most guide books, particularly those from the past, make wondrous claims about the climate of this part of southernmost Devon. It's generally true, particularly in comparison to the high and barren wastes of upland Dartmoor, to the north, that this area enjoys a more benign climate. There are several days in winter when it's possible to stroll around without recourse to sport heavy clothing. However, like most places, it has had its moments. The Great Blizzard of 1891, which started on 8 March that year, paralysed the county for some six weeks and this coastal patch did not escape its icy clutch. However there were those who considered that another blizzard ten years before that, in 1881, was far worse. Food became so scarce that siege prices existed. The stage coach, usually so reliable, however severe the storm, on this occasion was grounded for many days. At the height of the 1881 storm many of the boats on the beach at Torcross were blown away landing up in Slapton Ley! Life in the South Hams was not always quite as comfortable a place to be as the travel writers would have us believe!

The road, that is now known as the A379, was largely completed in its present form, in 1855, by the Turnpike Trustees under the leadership of Governor Holdsworth of Dartmouth. Until it was built this 20-foot high ridge was a cattle grazing ground. Despite the saline conditions, all sorts of things grew wild here. The most famous became quite a delicacy – sea kale. Its roots, if you'll excuse the pun, go back to 1775 when sea kale taken from Slapton Sands was cultivated in the garden of Mr Southcote, of Stoke Fleming, and then sold at Exeter market at the amazingly expensive price of half a crown per root, a week's earnings for many. Despite this those with the necessary wherewithal assured the fame of the Slapton sea kale spreading even farther afield. What Mr Southcote's gardener tried as a cooking experiment by boiling some of them turned out to be a 'nice little earner.'

Growing nearby, in the season, were foxgloves and marigolds, which were often referred to in the dialect forms of "Flopadocks" and "Drunkards".

The new road through these wondrous plants and vegetables was severely put to the test in January 1886 when an earthquake shook buildings in Torcross and caused much damage to the roof of the Green Dragon pub at Stoke Fleming. People living on the line between these two places rushed out of their houses at 10.20 one Monday morning. The tremors struck fear into some of the older residents who thought that the end of the world was nigh!

Strete, like Stoke Fleming, sits on top of a hill. In 1870 the spelling of the village's name changed from Street to Strete. This, apparently, was to avoid confusion with the Somerset "Street" near Glastonbury. As lots of post went awry, it was decided that the smaller one would transpose two letters.

Several of the houses enjoy tremendous views along Start Bay or towards the Daymark beyond the Dart. George Bernard Shaw also thought this a beautiful corner of England and stayed at a boarding house on Matthew's Point. There used to be a large house called 'The Retreat' where the Misses Pack and Moriarty used to run a home for run down clergymen, and their wives, who were in need of a rest from their labours. When Miss Pack died it was taken over by the Girls' Friendly Society. These and some of the other details were gleaned from a book written in the 1930s, *Strete Past & Present* by Marion F. Smithies. She almost named everyone who lived in this village at that time. Here is just one paragraph that is packed with little snippets of information and bits of relevant village small talk.

Next we must step across the road, looking out for motor cars and cycles for it is a dangerous corner, and on the opposite side is Mrs Somer's "Hartley Cottage", within a gate, and "Rushford" where Mrs Jarman and her little dog live. Next to this, on the Dartmouth road are three cottages in the old style. In the first is Mrs Harriet Tucker and her son "Jack", who is well known for his care of the churchyard, for his skill in managing a horse, and in winning prizes for his vegetables at the shows. Strete is proud to think that Mrs Tucker's grandson "Bert" Stone, whose mother was a war widow, stroked the

Dartmouth crew which won the all England Amateur rowing-race on the Thames in 1933, receiving the Duke of Bedford's Cup. Next door live Mr & Mrs Isaacs, the owner of the three cottages, and in the end one with the pretty garden Mr & Mrs Yalland. The great oak beams in their kitchen were once part of a ship which came ashore at Strete Sands.

It tells us of the gardener at the old coachhouse, near Strete Lodge, who was out chopping wood when the ground gave way. When he had landed and got his bearings he discovered that he had fallen into what was probably a smuggler's store. There was also details of how John Masefield, who became Poet Laureate, visited Strete for holidays when he was a young man. He stayed at Snails Castle, the home of the artists Mr and Mrs Yeats. Jack Yeats painted portraits of Slapton fishermen and also made grim and gruesome-looking scarecrows of sailor-men or smugglers for his garden. They were so scary that even some of the children were frightened by their appearance!

That little book is as local as one could wish, a bit like a street directory with soul. For those who own a copy and know the cottages and maybe some of their occupants, it is a lasting reminder of how things were in this small South Hams settlement at a moment in the village's evolution.

One of two communities in Start Bay to have been forced out of their original site was the 'Undercliff' village of Strete. It was a row of fishermen's cottages that clung to the cliff base "like swallows' nests". It was similar in appearance to Beesands and the original Hallsands, two villages farther south and closer to Start Point. These 'Undercliff' dwellings were not as conspicuous as those others. They were nestled among the verdant splendour of a vegetation consisting of trees and bushes. The beach must have been an impressive sight in the days when people lived there. *Down in the sands, which were much broader in those days, there would be rough boats made of wickerwork covered with skins of animals, and lobster pots and spears to strike at the big fish, and any other sea monsters.* (Marion F. Smithies, 1934)

Most fishermen will tell you, in no uncertain terms, that the fishing in Start Bay was much better in the past. In 1856 (and he'd have to be a very old fisherman to remember that year!) the fishermen of Strete and Torcross shared a catch of 100,000 mackerel in July, followed by a further 40,000 in November of that year. In those days migrating shoals of smaller fishes were an annual and expected catch. The fishermen kept a vigilant watch leaping into frantic action when they arrived.

There was a rivalry with the fishermen of Torcross that manifested itself in an annual race at sea. In 1857 the fishermen of Strete climbed into 'The Ranters' and battled with their opposition, from the other end of the beach, for the prize of a guinea. For many years Torcross Regatta was an annual event on the calendar with good money prizes on offer to winning boats.

However there have been days when the last place anyone would want to be was out on the briny in storm-battered Start Bay or perhaps out in a thick fog. Both types of weather have played havoc in the past... One of the oddest strandings ever to occur in Start Bay, many years ago, involved a submarine. She was making for Plymouth when she became enshrouded in a thick fog. The captain was amazed to have his vessel aground on what he thought was a sand bank some miles offshore. Imagine, then, the surprise that he had, after the mist cleared a little, when he saw a cyclist riding by! He had beached at Slapton Sands.

Charles Jose was a Belgian steamer of some 599 tons, which was carrying scrap iron from Antwerp to Llanelli in South Wales in December 1933. It made these headlines in the local press: "WRECK ON DEVON COAST – BELGIAN STEAMER'S CREW

RESCUED – SCENE LIT BY CAR LIGHTS – CAPTAIN'S WIFE BROUGHT ASHORE IN BREECHES BUOY." Those dreaded sea conditions that afflict this coastline when the easterly reigns supreme made life difficult for this vessel. The crew and the captain's wife were taken off, the Torbay Lifeboat arriving just in time to assist. Villagers with cars were asked to come and park along the beach in order to illuminate the scene enough for the rescue to be effected. Fortunately there were no injuries or loss of life. The stranded ship gave the locals and press photographers something to snap at for the days over Christmas. The locals, quick to earn a few bob, helped unload the scrap iron, which was then taken by road to a merchant in Kingsbridge. Much lighter, she was finally re-floated in early January 1934, free to resume her adventurous career on the high seas.

The area's biggest upheaval took place in the autumn of 1943, a dramatic and destructive episode that has its consequences to this very day. This particular area was generally regarded as a quiet backwater, the people who lived here, even in times of war, were content to live in a place still regarded as being behind the times. A lot of these folk probably had little idea that the countryside bore striking similarities to that of the coastline and countryside of the Cotentin Peninsular of Normandy. So similar was it that the powers that be regarded it as an essential place to practise invasion landings. No matter that this was an important agricultural area, with about three thousand people from small villages or outlying farms and hamlets. If Hitler was to be beaten everyone had to make sacrifices and this patch was one of a number commandeered for such uses.

It is well to put things into some perspective as now in the age of the motor car those people, of working age, who live in these places usually commute to larger centres of population for their work. However more than half a century ago villages like Blackawton, East Allington, Sherford, Stokenham, Chillington, Stokenham, Torcross, Slapton and Strete were far more self-sufficient than nowadays. For many who lived here a trip to nearby Kingsbridge, Dartmouth or Totnes, was something of an expedition that needed planning, and was not a journey undertaken frequently. So when the news broke that the Americans were coming and that within about six weeks they would have to be out of the district, lock, stock and barrel, for some it was an earth-shattering blow. They had, to all intents and purposes, already lost their coastline, it having been mined and barbed wired in the cause of coastal defence.

The last months of 1943 saw scenes of intense activity, the sort of exodus that has been seen in many other countries around the world but rarely in this country. Three thousand people had to up their roots, gather together their possessions, pets, poultry and other forms of livestock, and vacate their homes. Many had friends or relations just outside the district whilst some went farther afield never to return. The South West was almost filled to overflowing with evacuees from the big cities so those without the necessary connections were obliged to go over the hills and far away.

Some didn't survive the ordeal and it is conjecture whether the disruption hastened their demise – we shall never know.

What is known is that some 750 families were involved, who lived in an area of some 30,000 acres spread over six parishes. Compensation would be due in the shape of payments for a range of out of pocket expenses, before, during and after the evacuation. It was also clearly specified that compensation would also be paid for those whose properties sustained damage. This helped to cushion the blow for some of the evacuees.

The people had to be out by 20 December 1943. This was an area where the locals were more used to seeing people arrive to stay with them than going away themselves.

Consequently many families did not possess suitcases. And there were other practicalities that needed immediate attention, not least what do with all the cattle. The Women's Voluntary Service did some sterling and tireless work. Where the military were more concerned with the end result of a cleared, unpopulated large open air theatre for their rehearsals, the WVS were a shoulder to cry on, the coordinators orchestrating and being involved in it all in a bid to alleviate as much human misery as possible.

Devon can be a wet county at times and there is something definitely cussed about the whims of the weather. When dry conditions would be of help it will rain and vice-versa. The South Hams wet monsoon season ensured that the lanes ran red with mud creating conditions that were far from ideal for the great evacuation. If you have ever tried some of the steeper, narrower lanes, after prolonged heavy rain you will appreciate the problem. Local knowledge was also an invaluable commodity as all signposts had been taken down. Outsiders and those without a sense of direction found the lanes to be a veritable maze twisting this way, then next. Examine an O/S map and you will see for yourself!

Inevitably, of the number of churches in this area, each had their own particular treasures. Anything that could be removed was taken, which was just as well for some were in for some less than divine attention. Those items of value that could not be removed were sandbagged. Other internal bits and bobs were packed in straw and once the team from Exeter entrusted with the task had finished a church it was locked and made semi-secure with barbed wire. The Bishop of Exeter had a note affixed to the entrance of each church which read:

To our Allies of the USA

This church has stood here for several hundred years. Around it has grown a community, which has lived in these houses and tilled these fields ever since there was a church. This church, this churchyard in which their loved ones lie at rest, these homes, these fields are as dear to those who have left them as are the homes and graves and fields which you, our Allies, have left behind you. They hope to return one day, as you hope to return to yours, to find them waiting to welcome them home. They entrust them to your care meanwhile, and pray that God's blessing may rest upon us all.

Charles

Bishop of Exeter.

Towards the end of the evacuation period the entire area had assumed an almost surreal feel to it. Empty village streets resembled a scene from *High Noon* but this time the gun fight was to occur later. The fields and empty hills took on an eerie presence. What was traditionally a warm, friendly place where everyone always had a cheery greeting, was now a ghost town dowsed in Devonshire rain, the sounds of those strong Devonshire accents, that, at times, sound like those of Americans, were about to give way to the Real McCoy even though many weren't aware of the scale of what was about to happen. All that was left, as Christmas 1943 approached, were a few domestic animals still at large and a number of rats taking advantage of the situation to have a real bean feast and swell their numbers.

The tide had now changed. Instead of the drift away there was a real surge of personnel into the cordoned off area. Eisenhower and Montgomery were there and the people were aware of a massive scale of training operations, something was going to happen later that year. Eisenhower took over Sheplegh Court, just south of Blackawton, as his HQ. (After the war it became a naturists' hotel but later was converted to apartments.)

However there was no doubting the seriousness of all those involved in the occupation of this part of the South Hams for there were several full scale exercises where live ammunition was used. Inevitably there were losses like many fish in Slapton Ley, one minute swimming along without a care in the world, the next blown sky-high out of the water to rain down on the banks of the lake, onto the shingle bar. A large number of nesting birds were also killed, several years passing before their surviving relations had the confidence or nerve to return there to breed again.

A favourite port of call for people coming into this area was the Royal Sands Hotel, which stood about half way along the shingle bar close to the point where the road from Slapton village

reached the shore. There is a large car park now to stop people parking on the verges. In 1940, a year when the Ley had become a skating rink for its wildlife, having frozen over to a depth of several inches, the nearby hotel had been wrecked by land mines. 'Pincher' Luscombe is believed to have been the cause of the hotel's destruction for he apparently wandered into the prohibited area and triggered off six land mines, causing extensive but not irreparable damage to the various buildings. Whether or not he survived the crashing masonry is not known for 'Pincher' was a Jack Russell terrier who was never seen again. Originally it had been part of a conglomeration of buildings known as Slapton Cellars and a theory arose that it was connected by an underground tunnel to the Chantry in Slapton. The 'Royal' in its name is believed to have come from a mid-nineteenth century visit by

King Edward VII when he was a boy. Guide books state that it cost 8/6d per day (approx 43 pence) to stay at this famous fishing hotel in 1905, a tidy little sum in those days.

But it was the extent of the number of human dead that is the greater cause for regret for many hundreds of men died here in a number of ways. As is often the case the various disasters to occur in and around Start Bay were kept quiet at the time. A small hotel on the bluff above Torcross was used as a temporary headquarters by officers. A bomb that went astray destroyed it and killed all the young men who were in it.

Another major disaster involved many hundreds of young men who drowned on April 27/28 when nine German E-Boats appeared during a major exercise, "Operation Tiger". Seven LST's full of troops were being chaperoned by a single corvette, HMS *Azalia*, when they were attacked. There was total chaos in a confrontation that caused more deaths than the losses sustained by American troops on Utah beach during the D-Day landings. To place a precise figure on the actual number who died is impossible as estimates range from many hundreds to several thousand depending on which source you read or are prepared to believe. The aftermath was horrendous with bodies being plucked from the sea but many were never recovered. It is believed that all the ones found were taken to an American cemetery at Brookwood (Woking) in Surrey but there were a few folk who reckoned that there were mass graves in the fields near the Bay. However the consensus of opinion, by those who have lived there a life time, is that this is untrue. Some will go a step further and maintain that the major incident where so many were killed took place much farther out in Lyme Bay. They believe that few or no bodies were washed ashore along this strip of coast.

It is no small wonder that so many people have either written fact or fiction, or a mixture of both, about this troubled occupation. In this battle the Royal Sands Hotel was flattened and the roof was ripped off Stokenham Church.

D-Day, because of the planning and execution, was the success that was hoped for. Meanwhile the deserted, once more, evacuation area lay unpopulated save for US sentries guarding it. There were obvious scars in and on the landscape for in every sense of the word this had been a real battleground.

Slapton's church took a direct hit, the south wall being blown out. Tiny splinters of shrapnel had to be taken out of the pews. At Blackawton, farther inland, the blame had to be squarely placed at the feet of the occupying American troops: forty oil lamps gone, the only lighting this church enjoyed as it was without electricity in those days; Hymn and Prayer Books strewn widely over the whole church; knee-deep debris everywhere with the remains of the church organ

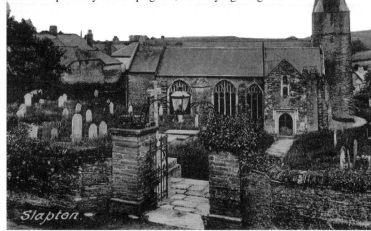

Slapton. -

left scattered over the graveyard. There was little reverence or respect paid to God's house by these offending troops. It is rumoured that Sir Walter Raleigh, that great Elizabethan seaman, married Elizabeth Throckmorton here. The later events would have probably made him turn in his grave! The vicar, upon returning, was naturally distressed by the wanton and wholesale destruction that he saw and it was only the keenness of his wife that made him move back to tackle the problem.

The pub's name at Blackawton was changed to the Normandy Arms.

A lot of the damage was mainly from vandalism but committed in that period of time after the Americans' departure but before the all clear for displaced locals to return. There are recorded stories of people sneaking back, past the watchful eyes of sentries, to visit their old farmhouses or cottages. Pleasantly surprised to see that the damage was minimal and easily put to rights they returned to their families with joyful news. However, when they officially got back home they were aghast at the damage that had occurred since their unofficial inspection. This was commonplace, a sad reflection that those who did this probably thought that they were not hurting the people themselves as full compensation was to be paid out.

There were shell-holes all over the district and cottages so damaged that they had been rendered unsafe for habitation. Some though came through unscathed needing little done to make them habitable once more. Some of the lovely coppices of woodlands, in the more sheltered valleys, suffered enormous damage. The lands in this area are generally fertile so when those who worked the land were taken away weeds of all sorts seized on the opportunity to run riot. But Mother Nature has a healing hand and once the human booby-traps had been removed she draped her mantle on the landscape to hide the scars of war.

Before the area could enjoy its rebirth much work had to be done to restore the roads, to get the public utilities back on stream. The drift back was gradual through the autumn of 1944 with an unreal atmosphere existing until the villages were topped up with their shops and pubs re-established once more.

The great loss in human life in those first six months of 1944 at Slapton has made this area a very sad, but special place. Every year there are visits from the relations and friends of those many hundreds of American troops who perished here all those years ago. To come here is a poignant experience for them. There are a few items for them to see on the pilgrimage to Slapton Sands, including the obelisk, where the Royal Sands Hotel once stood, shown here.

At Torcross, in the car park, between the Ley and the beach, is a Sherman Tank salvaged from the relatively shallow bed of Start Bay in 1984 by divers from Fort Bovisand, near Plymouth. Ken Small financed the operation, one that was not a simple straightforward task and one that gave him a lot of problems along the way. However, the placement of this memorial has obviously been appreciated by the thousands of visitors

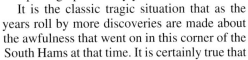

who photograph it every year.

It is the classic tragic situation that as the years roll by more discoveries are made about the awfulness that went on in this corner of the South Hams at that time. It is certainly true that the press maintained a veil of secrecy over major incidents with genuine headlines like "Boiled Lobster – story of an overcharge" hogging the front page when people were being blown to bits within miles of the editor's desk.

Leslie Thomas was an orphan at a Barnardo's home in Kingsbridge during the Second World War. In the late 1970s he wrote a fictional work, *The Magic Army*, based on the evacuation of this part of the South Hams and a television documentary in the summer of 1978 followed him in his research as he sat outside a pub at Blackawton trying to elicit information from some old locals. However his interviewees were a little camera-shy, one of whom was not very forthcoming about a meeting in November 1943 at Blackawton church to brief villagers on the evacuation of their area. It was only after minutes of cross-examination that the novelist discovered why local man, Percy Joint, couldn't answer such a specific question – he hadn't been to the meeting!

Writing novels rather than non-fiction, has its consequences. I'm told that each year many visitors, having read Leslie Thomas's book, turn up asking questions about fictitious places, people and events. This is the problem when a shandy of fact and fiction is concocted.

The village of Slapton is, like many in the South Hams, sheltered by being tucked into a fold in the hills, handily out of life's fast lane, and about half a mile

inland from the sands. Many villages of this area have a smaller population than they did a century and a half ago even though there are more houses now than then. Slapton had more than 700 residents in 1850 but that figure is now down to about 500. The village then had a brace of blacksmiths and bakers, a couple of corn millers, an octet of masons, a quintet of carpenters, a quartet of shopkeepers, a twin pack of tailors, a pair of publicans, an army of farmers and was well laced with shoemakers. In short there was plenty of work almost to the point of being self sufficient. Certainly the land surrounding the village is some of the richest in red Devon and has produced some of the finest flowers and vegetables ever grown in the county. The Anglo Saxons who began the first settlement at Slapton were good practical geologists who knew an excellent site when they saw one. This place also has an abundant supply of fresh spring water, some of the cottage names, even to this day, reflecting the number of wells in and around the village.

Go and have a look at Slapton today! It is a pretty village with attractive cottages. Artists often come and set up their easels to record the scene on canvas but it is not the working village that it was in the past.

The College of Chantry Priests has but few remains left other than the tower, after which a pub is named. It dominates the scene and has something of a history. Sir Guy de Brien, King Edward III's standard bearer, first founded a chantry here in 1373. He was also involved in helping to originate the Order of the Garter. The local slates were not of sufficient quality so the materials for this striking building were brought from quarries at Charleton, much nearer to Kingsbridge.

The idea was that priests would sing or pray for the founder or someone named by him. In this instance the chaplain, a number of priests and clerks did their daily divine duties in return for an annual allowance. On 31 May, each year, otherwise known as St Petronilla's Day, a funeral mass was sung for the founder and his wife.

It must have been a quiet and contemplative existence until 1545. Then Henry VIII decided to suppress all chantries and Slapton College was dissolved. The priests were paid off, the buildings were sold on but time and the elements leave us with an eighty-foot high tower and little else. Amen.

Poole near the village was the home of the celebrated Hawkins family. It is believed that one lady of the house had some fairly grand aspirations. Judith, wife of Sir John Hawkins' son, kept a roll of long red carpet that was unfurled before her, by two page boys, as she proceeded some three quarters of a mile to Slapton church. This wasn't so bizarre as a story from Sussex where a gentleman used cheeses as stepping stones when the track from the manor house to Chiddingley church was deep in mud!

Slapton's church, St James the Greater, with its medieval spire, is many centuries old, its fabric, as we have already seen, having been damaged in the D-Day preparations.

There are many whose first introduction to this area was by way of a visit to one of several residential centres. Slapton's old school is one of a number to be converted to such a use, the pupils coming to learn about a lot of the things mentioned in this book but by first hand experience – always the best way!

Slapton Ley (the Lower Ley) is the largest sheet, covering about 180 acres, of natural freshwater in Devon. At a maximum depth of about nine feet and an average one of about five feet it's not very deep. One day the natural silting process will probably see to it that there is no lake left at all, just an extensive area of reed beds. And perhaps its demise will see the end of the romantic story of King Arthur and the enduring saga of his famous sword. Some reckon that it was here, in balmy South Devon, where this great man chanced upon his wonderful weapon, which he wielded so wonderfully well. And when old 'Wart' was 'mort' his 'Excalibur' was thrown by Sir Bedivere into Slapton Ley to be caught, brandished thrice and drawn below by an arm "clothed in white samite, mystic, wonderful." Or maybe it was all just a very clever television commercial! Sadly Arthur probably predates the lake, which was only fully formed less than a thousand years ago.

When the Danes ravaged our shores it is likely they landed at Ireland Bay, once the coast now an inlet on the Ley. Possibly they attacked the fortified hill known as Slapton Castle only to be pelted by slingshot of flint gathered from the original coastal beaches.

The leys are extremely important for their variety of wildlife and the Slapton Field Centre is ideal for students of natural history. Herbert Whitley of Paignton, who originally set up the collection that has evolved into Paignton Zoo, set up a trust to manage the area as a Nature Reserve after his death. The Field Centre occupies a former hotel. The variety of species of fish in the Lower Ley are limited but roach, rudd, perch and pike are found in abundance. The latter, dubbed the freshwater shark, is the king predator with plenty on his menu here, as long as he doesn't mind having fish for starters. There are also many eels lurking in the mud at the bottom where there is a fine food supply available to them. In the 1950s there was a spate of stories about a monster eel that had been spotted on a number of occasions. It was believed to have been longer than the typical rowing boats used for fishing there.

For ornithologists the winter is probably the best season, the lesser-spotted tourist giving way to migratory flocks of birds. The Slapton year has its cycles and the number of suitably attired observers, complete with binoculars, is a reflection of the immense popularity of watching our feathered friends.

The road that runs along the top of the ridge between lake and sea is unusual. In 1934 S.P.B. Mais, in his book *Glorious Devon* described it like this, as seen when coming from the Dartmouth direction: *Almost at once you go down again to the open hedgeless road like no other in the kingdom. On both sides is water, the sea on your left breaking on the sand and shingle, the freshwater of Slapton Ley lying on your right where men fish from rowing boats with more than usual success. Reeds growing by the side of the lake are cut, stacked, and harvested like corn and used to make firm and most attractive hedges for all the neighbouring gardens. A little less than halfway along this strange shore stands Slapton Hotel, an inn of great fame among anglers.*

Stokenham is another village away from the coast. One of its residents is a man whose name would be instantly recognisable to those who read the credits that go up at the end of television programmes. Ed Welch has written many television theme tunes, a list that includes programmes like *Blockbusters*, *Knightmare*, *Catchphrase*, *Nelson's Column* and many others. He even wrote a song about that former children's television bunny, Gus Honeybun, now retired in the Cornish tourist attraction of Flambards. Ed has lived in the South Hams for many years and the scenery has inspired many of his compositions. Those who watch the BBC *Spotlight* programme will hear his composition that starts it off – the turning light being that of Start Point's lighthouse!

In the Queen's Silver Jubilee year of 1977 the residents of Stokenham buried a time capsule of small domestic items near the church, in the centre of the village. There is a strong community feeling and these villagers wanted to let people know, many centuries from now, what life was like when they were there. A time capsule from the earliest settlers of Stokenham, had there been one, would have told us that the settlement would have grown up at the top of a tidal inlet. As Slapton Ley wouldn't have been formed yet, Stokenham would have been closer to the coast.

Stokenham's church is a dominant landmark and in a guide book of 1905, with the

imaginative title of *Pearson's Gossipy Guide to South Devon*, it had this to say of it: *The Church is a picturesque old fifteenth-century building, dedicated to St Michael and All Angels, and is in Perpendicular style. It has a fine screen and a font of great age. As the church of Widecombe-in-the-Moor is called the Cathedral of Dartmoor, so this has been entitled the Cathedral of the South Hams.* (The same comment has also been made about the church at Malborough and the one at Modbury.)

Torcross is where the Lower Ley issues through a culvert under the road and cliff to percolate into the sea. It has already had several mentions, being more important than its small population would suggest. It is here that the A379 becomes shy of the sea and makes off on an inland corridor through the villages of Stokenham, Chillington, Frogmore and the two Charletons before reaching Kingsbridge after dallying with a creek or two along the way. It is also here, at Torcross, that the best bit of coast walking begins, although that is purely an opinion.

The village wraps itself around the southern end of the Ley, with many houses, hostelries and shops at lake level whilst many take advantage of the cliff-like slopes to be situated with fine views northward along Start Bay. A vantage point has been created a few hundred yards away; this is Torcross View Point and affords a remarkable vista. If you walk up the lane to it from Torcross you might like to take some time out and visit 'Harold's Field'. Here you are invited to come in, sit down and enjoy the view which, along the coast, extends as far as the Mew Stone, a few miles beyond the mouth of the Dart.

The village survives despite some of the storms that have tried their best to wreck it. In January 1979 enormous waves washed over the roofs of the houses that line the shore side of the settlement. Film crews shot down there and all the country were treated to the spectacle of monster waves breaking ferociously against this tiny community. Much

damage was done. Houses were flattened and flooded, the coastal defences were helpless in the face of so fearsome an easterly blast. As a temporary measure convoys of lorries brought lorry loads of boulders from the Plymouth area to protect Torcross and neighbouring Beesands from any further, immediate punishment. Since that terrible tempest a new sea wall has been carefully engineered so that the thrust of powerful waves is combated by the curved design. This way most of the wave energy is reduced.

Torcross needs its visitors and they come for the reasons that will have become apparent having read this far. They will, no doubt, be amused at some of the unusual road signs informing motorists to be aware of the presence of bird life. Most visitors have a soft spot for the ducks, geese and swans that accumulate in this corner of the Ley.

The countryside and coastline towards Start Point is very different to that encountered so far. If the tide is out or low it's possible to wearily walk along the shingle beach to Beesands, the next small community along the coast. However if it's in it's a case of upwards and onwards for the South Devon Coastal Path rises alarmingly from Torcross. Alternatively if you want to reach Beesands, Hallsands or Start Point the lazy man's way, then a detour through mainly, foot-on-the-brakes, narrow lanes, awaits you.

The walk is sometimes a muddy one along a well-worn path. In places it is possible to see large slabs of slate used as divides between fields. This was a common practice in many parts of the South Hams. These stones are known as 'Shiners', possibly because when damp they glint in the sunlight, but that's just my theory. The path climbs high with tremendous views to be enjoyed and detours slightly inland to skirt the enormous, but disused, Beesands Quarry. In the past it was a major source of slate, probably being the

source of many shiners and employed many people but today it lies forlorn and is overgrown in vegetation. Little is seen even though the path runs around its lip. But what has climbed up for an eternity has to go down again. The path now leads to a delightful spot where one should rest one's weary bones or calm one's shattered nerves depending on how one has got there.

I like Beesands very much. It has a pleasant feel about it but when it featured in the BBC's *Holiday* programme, many years ago, its caravan park came in for 'a bit of stick.' The park, on a narrow green strip sometimes referred to as 'Beesands Green' started in about 1958. It started from humble beginnings but the loveliness of this part of the world resulted in a high proportion of those coming once returning time and time again. Thus the caravan park grew until there were about 300 vans on site. For such a small community it was a Jekyll and Hyde affair as the narrow lanes to and from here were ill-equipped to cope with large numbers of vehicles on a daily basis. However, as the traditional occupations of fishing and farming experienced something of a decline the jobs created in association with the visitors was a Godsend. But someone, somewhere, had other ideas and the park closed in the mid 1980s giving back this small community its village green, but not exactly the sort one conjures up in the mind when that phrase is used. The village football pitch has seen some splendid soccer matches over the years, there never being a shortage of goal mouth incidents or goals. In a westerly wind this is one of the most sheltered sporting arenas in the county. For years Beesands, despite its lack of size, has turned out teams to play in the South Devon League.

Beesands is not the sort of place you drive through as the roads that go there go nowhere else. After the tortuous bends through the nearby hamlet of Beeson the silver shining sea at

Beesands is spotted. The coastal defences are an obvious feature, placed there to stop the village being wiped out like its neighbour of Hallsands, just a pleasant cliff walk down the coast, was many years ago.

A line of cottages is found along the sea front and amongst them a pub where ever-cheerful Cyril Courtenay has been for many years. When I was a teacher I often took fieldwork trips down to Start Bay and many is the time he has been a good Samaritan

allowing children and staff alike to dry their soaking wet clothes in his marvellous pub, the Cricket Inn. But don't be stumped by the name because it derives not from the sport but from some of its earliest owners who were called Cricket. And there's more… The pub's walls are a lesson in local history and geography for they contain pictures of the village from the past. It fits well with the description that C. G. Harper included in his book, *The South Devon Coast* in 1907.

Beesands has a perpetual air of rejoicing, for on every fine day the waste between the sea and the one row of fishermen's cottages flies its banner to sea and sky. It is only the domestic wash hung out to dry, but the effect is one of festival.

There is something Irish in the look and manners and customs of Beesands. The drying-ground of washing and of fishing nets is rich in old tins and brickbats, and is populated numerously with fowls, housed as a rule in decayed boats turned keel upward. They are the most trustful cocks and hens in the world, and follow the fishermen into the inn and the cottages like dogs.

A tourist not preoccupied with the arts would inevitably style this a 'miserable place,' a 'wretched hole,' or other things uncomplimentary; but to a painter, wanting atmosphere and utter unconventionality, it is delightful…

In those days it had another pub, the King's Arms, a few doors down towards Start Point and its own post office.

It would be wonderful to turn back the clock to the mid nineteenth century and visit these Start Bay fishing villages to see them in their heyday.

The fishermen and their families lived a tough existence depending on the harvests of the sea. They invariably kept specially trained Newfoundland dogs to help them land their catches, the currents running almost at a right angle to the shore always being a problem when coming ashore. Offshore is the Skerries Bank, a shallow, plentiful fishing ground that was the source of their livelihoods. But the fishermen needed to be adaptable because many species of fish were migratory keeping many a man on his toes in eager anticipation of a bumper catch. At different times various techniques were employed to catch cunning crustaceans, passing by pilchards or 'mazed' old mackerel and mullet. But despite the excitement generated by huge shoals of fish this was still a quiet backwater out of the mainstream of life where longevity was almost compulsory provided Davy Jones' Locker didn't beckon.

However, despite the peace of Beesands the community was shattered in the Second World War when it was bombed, seven people being killed as a result. Cyril still has the press cuttings, which interested visitors can examine upon request.

Again the option of walking or driving to the next village of Hallsands presents itself. The coast walk is really not too difficult provided that there have been no recent land slips to close it. On leaving Beesands there are some overgrown flat areas on the cliff top. These were allotments in the past where the local fishermen supplemented their families' diets by growing vegetables. The mild climate meant that something could be grown at almost any season. This stretch of coastline is one that I have often used when there has been a stiff westerly making walking an uncomfortable pastime in other parts. The shelter afforded by the cliffs and hills often means that it feels many degrees warmer here in such conditions, the chill factor not being a problem. The path, overhung with vegetation in a wet, warm summer climbs over Tinsey Head but as this is not a prominent headland it will

hardly be noticed. Ahead the ruined village of Hallsands awaits but with such dark ruins, camouflaged against dark coloured cliffs, the village will be difficult to define with the eye unless it is illuminated by the morning sunshine that often lights up Start Bay.

C. G. Harper came this way in 1907 to write his guide book to South Devon and had this to say of his passage from Beesands towards The Start: *A mile of climbing up cliff paths and scrambling down, and then across another scrubby bottom where the white campions grow, brings the adventurous stranger to Hall Sands, built into the tall dark cliffs, just as the house-martens plaster their nests against the eaves. The hardihood – the foolhardihood, if you like it better – that ever induced mortal man to build houses in this perilous position under the threatening eaves of the cliffs and on the margin of the waves can only be appreciated by those who look upon the place itself. It beggars description.*

The scene is one of a wild beauty, the cliffs rising dark and craggy overhead, draped thickly with ivy, the end of the street blocked with gigantic masses of fallen rock, and the sea at the very foot of some of the houses; with here and there a narrow strip of beach. But Harper was wrong to question the wisdom of those who chose to live there. They may have been simple fisherfolk but they weren't simple!

The story of the village, like that of the D-Day preparations, has filled pages in many a book, newspaper and magazine. It cannot be left out of this one either. For years school geography text books have used it as an example of the folly involved in tampering with nature's elements and of ignoring the constant warnings of a local population who had lived for many generations in close harmony with their surroundings. In hindsight it's easy to see why qualified engineers would take little notice of the moanings and groanings of humble fishermen. What did they know about the complex workings of the sea? Surely they were only out to cause as much fuss as possible?

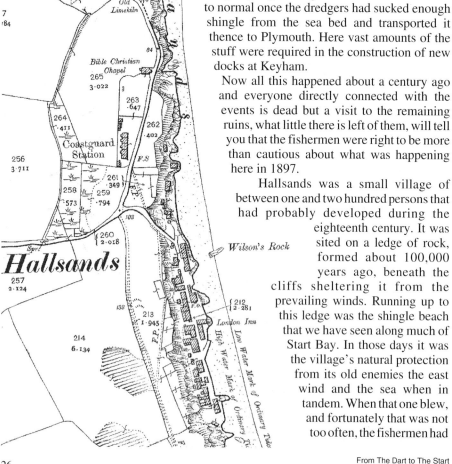

As far as the engineers were concerned nothing was going to go wrong and life would soon return to normal once the dredgers had sucked enough shingle from the sea bed and transported it thence to Plymouth. Here vast amounts of the stuff were required in the construction of new docks at Keyham.

Now all this happened about a century ago and everyone directly connected with the events is dead but a visit to the remaining ruins, what little there is left of them, will tell you that the fishermen were right to be more than cautious about what was happening here in 1897.

Hallsands was a small village of between one and two hundred persons that had probably developed during the eighteenth century. It was sited on a ledge of rock, formed about 100,000 years ago, beneath the cliffs sheltering it from the prevailing winds. Running up to this ledge was the shingle beach that we have seen along much of Start Bay. In those days it was the village's natural protection from its old enemies the east wind and the sea when in tandem. When that one blew, and fortunately that was not too often, the fishermen had an uncomfortable time. However their homes were safe, the high-ridged pebble beach well able to absorb the force of storm waves crashing in from the English Channel. The villagers of Hallsands had the perfect place to live with even some decent soil, on the cliffs, to grow vegetables. Life in the community was a sociable one with doors remaining open so that people mingled in a way that is not common these days. Even the chickens, that many kept, had no specific patch and wandered at will in and out of the various dwellings. These were as 'free range' as it was possible to get!

Any news of the outside world was most likely to come by sea. Passenger steamers, still something of a novelty around the coasts of Devon, often called at Hallsands whilst en route between Plymouth and Dartmouth. The attraction for them was the London Inn where refreshments were taken according to the time of day of their visit. The locally brewed, but notoriously potent, white ale was often consumed. A few pints of that heady brew was almost certain to guarantee a woozy trip back to port!

The shingle dredging operation began in 1897. In the four years up to December 1901 more than 650,000 tons of shingle were removed. The licence for dredging was then revoked but it was all a bit late. The beach that was Hallsands' protection had dropped so much that when easterlies occurred waves came right up to the rock ledge where the houses were now precariously located. The entire foreshore all the way to Beesands had changed and dropped dramatically.

Of course there were questions raised, even in Parliament. Compensation, although completely inadequate, was forthcoming. The influential Colonel F.B. Mildmay MP took up the cause of the fishermen. The dredging stopped, repairs to damaged sea walls were effected and the winter weather for the ensuing seasons more or less behaved itself. But the people of Hallsands knew that if certain conditions prevailed there would be major problems and they didn't have to wait too long. The winter of 1902/03 was a bad one. The sea wall in front of the London Inn collapsed and some properties were rendered

uninhabitable. But worse was to come. In September 1903 much of the London Inn, itself, was damaged along with the village street. The landlady was making tea, one afternoon, when the side of the house suddenly disappeared without warning, a heavy groundswell having wrecked this part of Hallsands. The old village of South Hallsands had to make do without an inn after that.

Later that year more damage was caused and a few of the villagers started leaving with no intention of returning. In the spring of 1904 another series of easterlies, some from the north-east, others from farther south, played havoc breaking windows and washing out more of the infill below and between the defences. The undermining process gnawed away at the tiny fishing village. All the time the cruel sea was preparing Hallsands for that final, knockout blow.

After a few years the villagers were divided between those who thought that the worst had been done and those who still prophesied the doom and eventual destruction of the village. But the years rolled by and although the fishing wasn't as fruitful, a sense of calm and security gradually returned. A series of typical winters with the westerlies huffing and puffing clean over the top of the cliffs presented no problems to Beesands or Hallsands until 1917 when the old, deadly combination of the dreaded easterly and high tides wreaked havoc.

On 26 January 1917, a strong north-easterly blew up and the village was in for a battering, the like of which it had never experienced before. The villagers were helpless as enormous waves crashed with immense power over their homes. Nothing could withstand the onslaught, waves coming down the chimneys to carry possessions off into the stormy night. It was a frightening experience for the villagers with four houses reduced to ruins before midnight. Many would have probably been drowned had there not been a lull in the storm at low water with just about enough time for all the families to scramble up the narrow cliff path to safety.

When the tempest had finally blown itself out and the high tides had subsided the villagers were left to survey the damage. In all twenty-nine homes were completely destroyed out of about thirty-seven. In the case of many not a single solitary stone remained, even the foundations had been washed away! Some that remained were beyond repair and, besides, the occupants didn't want to suffer the same fate again. Only one dwelling remained in a habitable condition, probably because it was slightly more elevated than the rest.

The villagers salvaged what they could but it wasn't much for most and none for some. Hardship followed for many Hallsands families. There were those who, having nowhere to go, slept amidst the ruins of the village whilst the others went to stay with families or friends. Five folk even shared a hayloft for several months.

The battle for compensation was a long one with the villagers' cause being championed by Colonel Mildmay, H. Ford, Richard Hansford Worth and A.E. Spender of the *Western Morning News*. Some familiar names also appeared on the committee set up to raise money. Locally there were the Prettyjohns from Hallsands, the Windeatts from slightly farther afield and Stephen Reynolds from Sidmouth. He was a scientist, turned fisherman, who had a talent for writing and his book *Poor Man's House* made him famous in the literary world. He, whenever possible, did his best to improve the lot of the fisherman, Hallsands being the sort of challenge that he would have relished.

Eventually, after years of fund-raising and compensation-seeking, a row of new houses called Fordworth Cottages were built in 1924, with two more added in 1932, at Greenstraight, a short distance from the old village. These were built on the hillside overlooking the former Hallsands lagoon and South Hallsands Beach. This was where crab pot makers had acquired the withies or reeds for their profession. There was an export trade in the fine pots they made as they were in widespread demand.

Elizabeth Prettyjohn, who had been born at the Cricket Inn, Beesands in about 1884, lived in the sole remaining house in the old village. She acted as a guide, for a great many years, to all the various curious visitors who came to see the village. I can remember, as a small child, having her pointing out things to us when we roamed the ever-diminishing ruins. Miss Prettyjohn passed away in 1964 but people still flock to the village, even though at the time of writing there is no access to it as the path that leads down the cliff has subsided. Hopefully, as this is such an important part of the area's heritage, an alternative way down to the ghostly gaunt ruins will be found.

It is a strange observation to make but it was the sea, when its general level was some fourteen feet higher than it is today, that originally was the architect of the platform where Hallsands developed. And it was the sea, again, that took Hallsands away when the protective ridge of shingle had been depleted by man, allowing it to return with a vengeance.

Some of the cliff top buildings are also in danger of disappearing down to join the mermaids as well. The chapel, which probably hasn't got a prayer of surviving, is teetering and a couple of holiday lets have got more than just a room with a view. However, nearby the Hallsands Hotel stands defiantly on its bluff, safe in the knowledge that nothing much has disappeared beside it since at least 1946. An old photo from that year bears this out. The hotel, a dominant landmark for walkers approaching from the Torcross direction, was built when the London Inn was destroyed in 1903. It took three years to build, opening for business in 1906, strange as it may seem, as a 'coaching inn'.

Two of its previous owners packed in the high life of running a shop in London to take over here. In their twenty-two years of ownership they attracted some of their old friends down to Devon. These included Danny La Rue and Larry Grayson and for years signed photos of these as two young fresh-faced lads adorned the walls. But times change and doors close! The Hallsands Hotel has changed direction and since 1980 specialises in diving holidays, the shallow, protected waters of Start Bay ideal for this pursuit.

The coastal path has been diverted between South and North Hallsands, a long flight set of steps going behind the Hallsands Hotel instead of precariously in front of it.

All books about this area relate the true tale of a young girl who became the Grace Darling of Start Bay in 1917. Perhaps she was even braver for whilst Grace, the grown up daughter of a lighthouse keeper, had her father with her when she rescued nine men from the *Forfarshire* during a storm in 1838, twenty-year-old Ella Trout only had her ten-year-old cousin as company whilst out fishing off Start Point. She saw a sinking tanker, about a mile away, which had been torpedoed by a German submarine. Immediately, she lowered her sails, got out her oars and set off for the stricken vessel. Whilst negotiating the wreckage she saw a young man whom she rescued and resuscitated, despite the real risk of being attacked herself. For this brave deed she was awarded an OBE. The parents of the young man were so grateful that they gave her a cash reward. The money was used to part finance the building of what became, in 1933, Trout's Hotel, now holiday flats, the large building at the top of the path down to the ruined village of Hallsands. Eight more of the crew were picked up by a Salcombe motor boat that had also been fishing there.

Although it is the brilliant white lighthouse that catches the eye as Start Point is approached, one can hardly fail to notice the giant masts on the cliffs above Hallsands. These appeared in the late 1930s, the BBC having decided to open a studio and a transmitter to improve the quality of their broadcasts in the West of England. It was officially opened in June 1939 by the Duke of Somerset and enabled people from Cornwall to West Sussex to get better reception. At the same time another was opened at Clevedon in Somerset to boost the northern side of the south west peninsular. The choice of Start Point, on such high cliffs away from centres of population, was an excellent one. From the vicinity there are tremendous views particularly towards Dartmoor.

The coastal path from Hallsands to Start Point is a gentle but steady climb. The only obstacle, apart from an occasional stile (misery for those with little or no coordination!) are some trees that the path passes beneath on its long haul upwards. These are all blown into the same angle but not by the prevailing winds as some guide books state! These are the victims of that phenomenon known as a sea breeze.

One of the quirkier reasons for organising this book in the way that it has been done has been so that I can finish at The Start! It is a wonderful place to round things off. To stand on one of its many rocky pinnacles, on a fine day, is a tremendous experience. Almost all the places that we have visited along the way are in view in an orgy of bays and bars, lovely lagoons and colourful cliffs.

Start Point has its own history. Its name derives from an Anglo Saxon word that means 'a tail'. Although this is not quite as far south as we can go in Devon, nearby Prawle Point claiming that honour, people have likened this southern tip of the county as being similar in a number of ways to its Cornish counterpart, The Lizard. Descriptions of The Start like to play on the appearance of this arete-like promontory to that of a monster. An edition of the *Cornhill Magazine*, long ago, had this to say of it: *The Start with its long tongue of rock, a warted and horrent tongue like that of some primeval dragon, closes the coast of Devon on the south-east.*

Old Harper described it thus: *The Start projects far out to sea, a dark mass of gneiss rock with quartz veins. It is in the uncomfortable shape of a razor-backed ridge, with demoniacal-looking humps, spires, and spires of iron-hard rock, ranging from prominences like the vertebrae of a crocodile's back to sharp points in the likeness of hedge-stakes.*

Its lofty perches became the grandstand for hundreds of people who gathered here in 1588 to watch Drake, and his fleet of relatively small ships, engage of the larger galleons of the Spanish Armada in one of the greatest episodes in our maritime history.

My friend, Raymond B, Cattell, started this book off with his visit to the Dancing Beggars. We will admit now that he managed to get away from his temporary exile on one of those painful points and managed to encounter several of the other places that we have covered in this book, including the Start…

We …set a straight course for Start Lighthouse. For all sailors in tiny craft – and even in big ones, as I have heard a cruiser gunner declare – the rounding of The Start is an experience in itself. For us it was also an achievement, equivalent to a big vessel's rounding of the Horn. For it is the haunt of a fierce tidal race, which in rough weather spreads a dread regiment of enormous white horses two or three miles out to sea. Even in the calmest weather the surface of the sea is twisted and tortured as by a far-flung whirlpool and from which the maddest whisperings and groanings rise in the still air. Sailors swear that the spirits of drowned seamen meet here. If so they must be expiating a peculiarly wicked life. Perhaps among them is that "Henri Muge, a pirate of the sea" who, according to local records, was hanged upon Start Point for all sailors to behold.

To make a detour around the race, far out to sea, did not appeal to me; better to try slip past near the shore and risk the rocks. Then I told Jean what to expect. It was well that I did, for even so she confesses her heart sank at the sight of the first whale-backed roller that rushed us. It was incredible to see those rollers rise out of the dead calm, oily sea. They came at us with a curious sideways motion, feinting like a boxer. Jean looked longingly at the little lane that runs round the firm cliff-side to the dignified white lighthouse, and remarked that a coastguard was watching our progress with an interested eye. For a few minutes we had an exhilarating tussle – no roller actually broke in our vicinity – and, owing to our clinging to the coast we were soon out of it.

The Start was passed! Its massive outline, built in hard gneiss rock and shining quartz, serrated like the scaly back of some prehistoric monster, closed the view behind us. Before us was the almost equally rugged Peartree Point – a windswept waste on which I am sure no pear tree would consent to grow.

And not all those who have tried to round this promontory have succeeded for the history book is littered with tragic episodes of shipwrecks. There are numerous examples of vessels foundering here despite the presence of the lighthouse. Ray Cattell referred to the souls of drowned seamen meeting here, some perhaps from the wrecks of the aptly named *Spirit of the Ocean*, *Gossamer*, *Lalla Rookh* and the steamship *Marana*, these being just some of Start Point's recorded victims. The first of these listed went aground between The Start and Lannacombe in March 1866. Of a crew of thirty only two survived.

Two ships carrying tea have gone aground on these inhospitable cliffs. The *Gossamer* perished in 1868 when thirteen of her crew were lost out of a ship's complement of thirty one. Five years later the *Lalla Rookh,* carrying 1300 tons of tea and 60 tons of tobacco, wrecked near Prawle Point, the currents eventually sweeping the cargoes into Start Bay. Mounds of tea eleven feet high appeared on Slapton Sands, thereby putting an entirely new meaning into the phrase 'a storm brewing'!

The most dramatic of these was the sad plight of the *Marana*, which was caught up in the much written about Great Blizzard of 1891. The storm had begun with a vengeance on 8 March and the *Marana*, which had got into trouble, approached The Start the next day. As night drew to a close the scene at Start could only be described as wild with violent conditions prevailing. The lighthouse keeper's wife was peering out of a window at the great snow flurries when she thought she caught a glimpse of a vessel but before her fears could be confirmed the steamship had gone. The crew abandoned ship in Lannacombe Bay, climbing with great difficulty into their lifeboats. One accommodated twenty-two of them whilst a smaller one took the remaining four crew members. Because of the surf at Lannacombe they were driven farther west but their lifeboat was smashed to pieces on Mag Ledge near Prawle. Only four men lived to tell the horrendous tale of what it was like to be completely at the mercy of the elements.

But we want to finish the book on a lighter note and it is the brightest light that shines along this coast that brings our brief look at this length of coastline to an end at The Start.

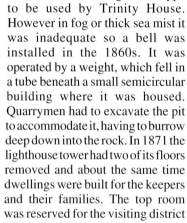

The white lighthouse has been in view most of the way. Visited by many people over the years, it is not possible any more for the light has been automated. In the past visitors climbed heavenwards up the many steps to the light where a guided talk was an 'enlightening' experience.

James Walker designed the lighthouse, which was opened in 1836. At the time gothic architecture was in fashion, Start Point with its battlemented parapet in line with this trend. Two white lights were originally exhibited, of which one revolved and the other acted as a fixed mark for the Skerries Rocks. This was the first light of its type to be used by Trinity House. However in fog or thick sea mist it was inadequate so a bell was installed in the 1860s. It was operated by a weight, which fell in a tube beneath a small semicircular building where it was housed. Quarrymen had to excavate the pit to accommodate it, having to burrow deep down into the rock. In 1871 the lighthouse tower had two of its floors removed and about the same time dwellings were built for the keepers and their families. The top room was reserved for the visiting district superintendent, a man from Penzance and a 'leading light' in this organisation.

We have now travelled the short distance 'From The Dart to The Start'. We have seen the folly of fellow men, witnessed episodes of great importance and others more trivial perhaps hardly worthy of a mention. But as we all know life is a merry old mix of tedium, trauma and tempest so I hope that this small literary offering helps to convey an impression of what this wonderful part of Devon is all about.